COMMUNITY WORKERS

An Electrician's Job

PATRICIA DAWSON

Cavendish
Square

New York

Published in 2015 by Cavendish Square Publishing, LLC
243 5th Avenue, Suite 136, New York, NY 10016

CPSIA Compliance Information: Batch #WS14CSQ

All websites were available and accurate when this book was sent to press.

Library of Congress Cataloging-in-Publication Data

Dawson, Patricia.
An electrician's job / Patricia Dawson.
pages cm. — (Community workers)
Includes index.
ISBN 978-1-62712-993-0 (hardcover) ISBN 978-1-62712-994-7 (paperback) ISBN 978-1-62712-995-4 (ebook)
1. Electricians—Juvenile literature. 2. Electricity—Juvenile literature. I. Title.
TK159.D39 2015
621.319'24092—dc23
2013050643

Editorial Director: Dean Miller
Editor: Amy Hayes
Copy Editor: Cynthia Roby
Art Director: Jeffrey Talbot
Designer: Douglas Brooks
Photo Researcher: J8 Media
Production Manager: Jennifer Ryder-Talbot
Production Editor: David McNamara

Printed in the United States of America

Contents

Electricians make sure your lights turn on.

Electricians help bring **electric power** to your home.

This room needs a new light.

A light has **wires** that make it work.

7

I tie the wires together.

First I tie the red wires.

Then I tie the black wires.

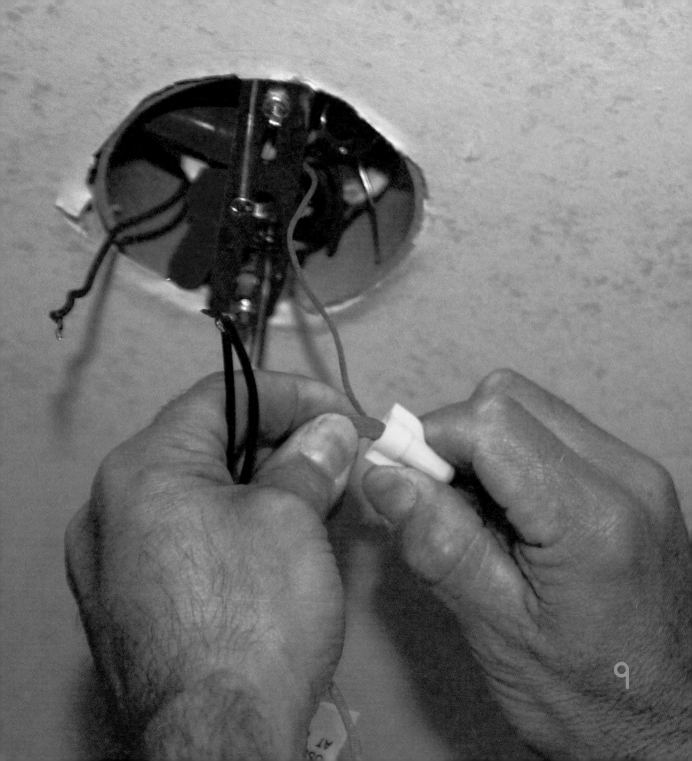

9

I put in a **lightbulb**.

I put the cover over the lightbulb.

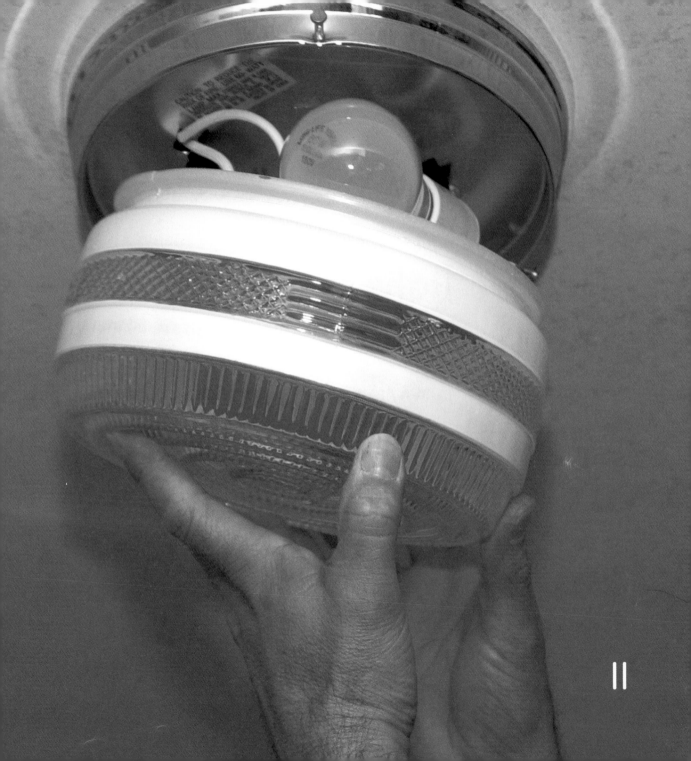

I put in a **light switch.**

The switch will make the light turn on and off.

13

Some houses use **circuit breakers.**

I check to make sure each circuit is working correctly.

15

This circuit has been **tripped**.

I switch the circuit off and on.

I fix the circuit.

I turn on the light.

It works!

The room is nice and bright.

19

Electric power can be dangerous, but people use it every day.

I like bringing light to your home.

I like being an electrician.

21

Words to Know

circuit breakers (**sir**-ket **brae**-kerz) switches that turn off if there is a problem with electricity in your home

electric power (eh-**lek**-trik **pow**-er) a form of energy that produces light

electricians (eh-lek-**trih**-shuns) people who work with wires and electric lights

lightbulb (**lyt**-buhlb) a type of bulb that gives off light

light switch (**lyt swich**) something that helps you turn a light on or off

tripped (**tripd**) turned off

wires (**wy**-erz) thin pieces of metal that carry electric power to a light

Find Out More

Books

Electricians
by Cecilia Minden, Childs' World

Switch On, Switch Off
by Melvin Berger, HarperCollins

Young Discoverers: Batteries, Bulbs, and Wires
by David Glover, Kingfisher

Website

Career Information: Electrician
www.education.com/reference/article/career-information-electrician/

Index